Online Services and Lab Glass: Forensic Investigation and Cloud Computing

Online Services and Lab Glass: Forensic Investigation and Cloud Computing

By

SARON MESSEMBE OBIA

Vij Books India Pvt Ltd
New Delhi (India)

Published by

Vij Books India Pvt Ltd
(Publishers, Distributors & Importers)
2/19, Ansari Road
Delhi – 110 002
Phones: 91-11-43596460, 91-11-47340674
Mob: 98110 94883
E-mail: contact@vipublishing.com
Web : www.vijbooks.in

ISBN: 978-93-93499-26-4 (Hardback)

ISBN: 978-93-93499-50-9 (Paperback)

ISBN: 978-93-93499-51-6 (ebook)

DEDICATED TO

Almighty God and Ms. Philomena O'Grady, Forensic Criminologist

"Many people, especially ignorant people, want to punish you for speaking the truth, for being correct, for being you. Never apologize for being correct, or for being years ahead of your time. If you're right and you know it, speak your mind. Speak your mind. Even if you are a minority of one, the truth is still the truth."

– Mahatma Gandhi.

CONTENTS

Abbreviations

ACPO	Association of Chief Police Officers.
BEAC	Central Back of Central African States.
CSP	Cloud Service Providers.
DFRW	Digital Forensics Research Conference.
DDoS	Distributed Denial of Service.
DFaaS	Digital Forensics as a Service.
EBS	Elastic Block Store.
FDE	Full Disk Encryption.
HPC	High performance computing.
ICCID	Integrated Circuit Card Identifier.
IT	Information Technology.
IaaS	Infrastructure as a Service.
IoT	The Internet-of-Things.
IPsec	Internet Protocol Security.
M&A	Mergers and Acquisitions.
MFS	Mobile Financial Services.
MTN	Mobile Telephone Network.
MTOs	Mobile Telephone operators.

NIST	National Institute of Standards and Technology.
NTFS/FAT	New Technology File System/File allocation table.
POR	Proofs of Retrievability.
PaaS	Platform as a Service.
PIN	Personal Identification Number.
PUK	Personal unlocking keys.
RAM	Random access memory.
SSO	Single sign-on.
S3	Simple Storage Service.
SaaS	Software as a Service.
SMBs	Small and Medium Businesses.
TBML	Trade-Based Money Laundering.
TOR	The Onion Router.
USB	Universal Serial Bus.
VI	Virtual Introspection.
VPN	Virtual Private Network.

Acknowledgement

The guidelines on the handling, collecting and preservation of digital evidence to support investigations, is drawn from a policing document, developed by International Criminal Police, after review and assistance from security agencies in Europe.

I wish to mention and thank the following persons, whose valuable input has helped to create security awareness, through conferences, which has trained experts in the domain of security studies; Dr. Daniel Ekongwe, Regional Director of the Pan African Institute for Development West Africa (PAID-WA), Buea, Cameroon, Mr. Wilson Mengole and Mr. Tata Wahri Derek.

I would also like to express my sincere gratitude to Mr. Tamfuh Bright, Mr. Charles Ebune and Mme. Modika Fembe Hilda, for their financial assistance, and to all information technology management experts.

EXECUTIVE SUMMARY

Globalization era presents a serious challenge to law enforcement agencies, financial regulators, and forensic investigators in particular. The emergence of Cloud computing in Information Technology (IT) phenomenon, which help organizations procure, deploy and manage physical IT infrastructure to host their software applications, has been under menace by cybercriminals. Organizations are increasingly deploying their infrastructure into remote, virtualized environments, often hosted and managed by third parties.

This development has significant implications for digital forensic investigators, equipment vendors, clients, as well as corporate compliance. Much of digital forensic practice assumes careful control and management of IT assets (particularly data storage) during the conduct of an investigation.

Chapter one provides a brief introduction to cloud computing and digital forensic. From a social perspective to criminal ideology. It further exposes on core elements for cloud computing, benefit and challenges. However, out pins, the difficulty of regulating the cyber space.

Technological innovation, forensic and encryption are aspects developed in chapter two. More so, technical issues relating to digital forensics as well as, sources and nature of evidence are discussed for proper understanding for the criminal justice system and judiciary.

This work summarizes the key aspects of cloud computing and analyses on the adoption of digital forensic procedures necessary for the growing menace. Several new research challenges addressing this changing context are also identified and discussed.

One of the most essential aspect of this work, is simulation and investigation of criminal activities using cloud. An example of case 009 with investigation in Xaas environments is exploited. Thereby concluding on how to secure network communication.

Chapter four provides a clear narrative on collection and handling of digital evidence for law enforcement officers. It also out pins, the procedure for handling digital evidence of criminal acts. Nevertheless, the work is a hand book for law enforcement officers and the criminal justice system.

Chapter One

Introduction

The internet has become the 'new base' where states, transnational actors and corporate organizations fight to secure data or privacy, which is increasingly weaponized. Those involved in the 'game' are; hackers, cybercriminals, forensic investigators, financial accountants and IT specialists. Some scholars argued that cloud computing is the best approach in securing data or information, though no one can affirm this stance, with the proliferation of digital tools which facilitates hacking of organization and the injection of ransomware in systems of profiled companies, all these for financial motives.

According to Cheka (2018), the regulation of financial services in a globalized world is connected to law and economics. However, it is argued that 'a rational system of law played a crucial role in economic development … by allowing individuals to order their transactions with some predictability' (Cheka, 2018). This collaborates with the fact that law guarantees economic interests and 'economic interests are among the strongest factors influencing the creation of law'.

In today's globalized world, the information, speed and convenience provided by digital technologies has enhanced the volume of economic and financial activity that monetary authorities that are not alert and fail to constantly adapt to these developments could simply become irrelevant.

Digital forensics is a vital domain of almost every criminal investigation, given the amount of information available and the opportunities offered by electronic data to investigate and provide evidence of a crime. However, it's sometimes challenging to experts during criminal proceedings, for the fact that, most electronic pieces of evidence are often considered with the utmost suspicion and uncertainty, although, on occasions are justifiable.

Nevertheless, the exceedingly distinct and dynamic characteristics of electronic data, in addition to the current legislation and privacy laws, remain a challenging factor for rendering evidence in the criminal jurisdiction. Most Sub Saharan African countries encounter such challenges.

Forensic science is defined as the exploitation of scientific or technical approaches for the identification, collection, analysis, and explanation of evidence in legal proceedings, including several disciplines, each providing techniques and procedures. Notably, digital forensics is one of the primary domains, given that all forensic sciences use valid principles and methods in the evaluation of evidence that is labelled as scientific evidence. However, the evidence must be empirical, as it provides support to either accept or counter a hypothesis and conclude on the guilty vs non-guilty outcome.

For actual evidence, it is essential that it can be explained and justified through systematic and experimental methods. The strength of any empirical approach relies upon the results of statistical analysis and the appropriateness of the trial and controls in that domain. Accordingly, standards used to check the validity of scientific evidence may vary as per the field of forensic examination.

In developed and in developing countries, social media evidence is a new paradigm for criminal proceedings, both for traditional and for cybercrimes. However, it also raises unique legal and technical challenges for digital forensics. As trials involving social media evidence are increasing each day, and legal proceedings on identity theft.

According to various surveys, in 2012, there were 689 published cases where social media data was presented as evidence, and further highlighting that from 2015 this practice has been quickly increasing[1]. However, in 2016, 14,000 decisions were reported for the 12-month period in the United States, and among these, 9,500 cases were vastly reliant on social media data as evidence.

Investigators are attracted to social media due to the ubiquitous, personal and footprint like nature of the data and develop kin attention to new software used by criminals. A treasure trove of proofs created by the suspect, or the victim, would be favourable if not gratefully received by detectives. Therefore, if they manage to investigate the proofs correctly for their value and potential, it might offer exceptional support in the criminal investigation process. The metadata accompanying the content and other information on social networking sites likewise holds enormous potential to assist in investigations[2].

Moreover, social media data is readily available and accessible to use as evidence for litigation purposes and investigations (sent mails, pictures, just to name but these). The published contents on social media along with an associated timestamp are often used to locate the whereabouts of an individual; could help to corroborate an alibi or might be suggestive of some prior or recent criminal activity.

1 http://xml.jips-k.org/full-text/view?doi=10.3745/JIPS.03.0095

2 Ibid 1

Recently, Cloud forensics has become a significant element in electronic investigations; to locate digital data involved in a crime, and saved in the cloud (virtual storage). The acquisition and analysis of forensic data hosted in the cloud environment are problematic. Many of the issues that arise are due to highly distributed and complex cloud architecture. Other reasons include the multi-tenant usage model, virtualization and the volatile nature of the data itself.

Also, privacy issues are a tremendous concern. Therefore, these problems emphasize the need for attention and the creation of legal and technical frameworks. The already established practices in digital forensics are at this stage, not applicable to the cloud environment, such as searching, and the collection of data, due to the lack of individual ownership of devices and data stored in the cloud.

Information Technology and Digital Shadows

Every year thousands of software are developed, and criminals create new strategies to be invisible when typing on the keyboard. One of the major aspects in contemporary criminal trends is inadequate expertise or massive skills gap, at one time, an investigator needed to understand the NTFS/FAT file system and associated file format, and that would help them to find contraband content.

The 21st century requires investigators to understand network protocols; different operating systems (such as iOS, Android, Mac, and so on); memory analysis (forensics investigation); cyber-attacks (DDoS, and SQL Injection); penetration testing; ransomware; traces of digital artifacts on the internet; and so on. It is thus difficult for investigators to keep up-to-date with the complete picture of the increasingly complex nature of our digital footprint.

Cloud computing technologies provides new techniques to organizations to ensure security of their Information Technology (IT) infrastructure. The shift to cloud computing involves replacing much of the traditional IT hardware found in an organization's data centre (including servers, network switches and air conditioning units) with virtualized, software services, configured for the particular needs of the organization. Services which can be hosted and managed by the user organization, or by a third-party provider. However, the software and data comprising the organization's application are usually stored across many different locations, potentially with a wide geographic distribution.

The market for cloud services have expanded at a geometric rate, during the last decade. This confirms Gens speculation on spending on cloud services up to 30% in 2011 (Gens, 2010) and statistics of the Gartner press forecast cloud service worldwide revenue to reach $68.3 billion in 2010, an increase of 16.6% from the 2009 revenue of $58.6 billion, and support the claim that cloud service revenues will reach $148.8 billion in 2014 (Pring, Brown, Leong, Biscotti, Couture, Lheureux, Frank, Roster, Cournoyer, & Liu, 2010). Many Small and Medium Businesses (SMBs) are continuing to exploit three or more cloud services (Kazarian & Hanlon, 2011).

The Core Element for Cloud Computing

1. Virtualization.

Virtualization is the key element for the implementation of cloud computing. Cloud Computing is defined as a pool of virtualized computer resources. Based on this Virtualization, the Cloud Computing paradigm allows workloads to be deployed and scaled-out quickly through the rapid provisioning of virtual machines or physical machines[3].

A Cloud Computing platform supports redundant, self-recovering, highly scalable programming models that allow workloads to recover from many inevitable hardware/ software failures (Paul, A. et al. 2012). A Cloud Computing platform is more than a collection of computer resources because it provides a mechanism to manage those resources[4].

In a Cloud Computing platform, software is migrating from the desktop into the "clouds" of the internet, promising users anytime, anywhere access to their programs and data. The concept of cloud computing and how virtualization enables it offers many innovative opportunities to make the cloud environment more dynamic and versatile.

VMware solutions are engineered and integrated to equip the cloud with a unique combination of benefits. Virtualization is the essential catalyst for cloud computing[5]. We can see that by the following process: Firstly, the user requests an application resource in a symbolic form (via URL). In addition, the cloud computing environment fields the request and assigns resources to the task. The resources are loaded with the required software and finally, the address of the resources is returned to the user and the application interaction proceeds.

As this sequence shows, the most critical requirement for cloud computing is that users have a virtual view of their applications and should never refer to an application resource with a static address. Doing so would prevent the cloud

3 https://eudl.eu/proceedings/cloudcomp/2009

4 IEEE Transactions on Computers. Volume: 62, Issue: 6, June 2013. https://ieeexplore.ieee.org/document/6509887/similar#similar

5 https://evantageit.com/cloud-computing/

from allocating resources flexibly. Since all cloud computing models must support a virtualized "front-end" interface to users, the management style of their virtual resources may be very different from one implementation to another.

2. Server-Virtualization.

The virtualization process within cloud computing system is divided into two sections; the front end and the back end. They connect to each other through a network, usually the internet. The front end is the client side (or the user end). The back end is the "cloud" section of the system.

The front end includes the user's computer and the application required to access the cloud computing system[6]. It's necessary to note that, all cloud computing systems do not have the same user interface. Despite the variety of services, Web-based email programs leverage existing Web browsers like Internet Explorer or Firefox. There exist other systems with unique applications which provide network access to clients.

On the back end of the system are the various servers and data storage systems that create the "cloud" of computing services[7]. Every application operates with a dedicated server to execute or perform a task. A central server administers the system, monitoring traffic and client demands to ensure the transmission of every request on the browser. This is done by the application of set of rules called protocols and uses a special kind of software called middleware. Middleware allows the computer systems connected in the network to

6 Ibid

7 Paul, A. et al 2012. Cyber Forensics in Cloud Computing. Computer Engineering and Intelligent Systems. Vol 3, No.2, 2012. https://iiste.org/Journals/index.php/CEIS/article/viewFile/982/902/

communicate with each other and exchange data (Paul, A. et al 2012).

Usually, the servers do not run at full capacity, which means that there is unused processing power going to waste. It is possible to overcome this problem by making a physical server act as if it is actually multiple servers, each running with its own independent operating system. The technique is called server virtualization. By maximizing the output of individual servers, server virtualization reduces the need for more physical machines. This helps in handling large amounts of loads which facilitates in scaling up and down of resources provided by the cloud.

A cloud computing company hosting several clients, will likely demand for more storage space. Some companies require hundreds of digital storage devices. Cloud computing systems need at least twice the number of storage devices it requires to keep all its clients' information stored. That's because these devices, like all computers, occasionally break down. A cloud computing system must make a copy of all its clients' information and store it on other devices. The copies enable the central server to access backup machines to retrieve data that otherwise would be unrecoverable.

Benefit of Cloud Computing.

1. **Supportive nature to organization.**

Technological evolution has changed the services, procedure, flexibility and efficiency of organization, because of the use of cloud computing. Virtualized services provide greater flexibility over an in-house physical IT infrastructure, because services can be rapidly re-configured or scaled to meet new and evolving requirements without the need to acquire new and potentially redundant hardware. However, the use of cloud computing equally minimizes the costs of providing

IT services, by eliminating redundant computing power and storage, reducing support requirements and reducing fixed capital commitments. Khajeh-Hosseini et al. found that a 37% cost saving could be obtained by an organization who chose to migrate their IT infrastructure from an outsourced data-centre to the Amazon Cloud (Khajeh-Hosseini, Greenwood, & Sommerville, 2010).

Challenges of Cloud Computing.

A. Socio-economic challenge.

One of the primary use of technology is for security, fast transmission of information, preservation of critical data. Cloud computing is a password for the 21st century because of the security it provides not only to organizations but also to individuals. However, the use of cloud computing presents significant challenges to users of clouds, as well as regulatory and law enforcement authorities.

Following Detica (2011) estimation in relation to cybercrime, appealing to cost the British economy £27 billion per year in future, with businesses accounting for nearly £21 billion of losses, largely due to the theft of intellectual property and espionage. This correlates with modern warfare, where data has been weaponized, and users of cloud computing services and other technologies are exposed to hackers, ransomware, and identity fraud.

The major menace is that of confidentiality and private data of organizations which though processed through cloud computing (Butler, Heckman, & Thorp, 2010) are still vulnerable. For example; Botnet attacks on Amazon's cloud infrastructure (Amazon Web Services, 2009) and breach of the Gmail email service by (alleged) Chinese hackers (Blumenthal, 2010) illustrates that cloud computing platforms are already a target for malicious activities.

1. Digital forensic investigation.

With the increasing demand for using the power of the cloud for processing sensible information and data, enterprises face the issue of Data and Process Provenance in the cloud. Digital provenance, meaning meta-data that describes the ancestry or history of a digital object, is a crucial feature for forensic investigations (Birk, 2011). In combination with a suitable authentication scheme, it provides information about who created and who modified what kind of data in the cloud. These are essential aspects for digital investigations in distributed environments such as the cloud.

Unfortunately, the aspect of forensic investigations in such distributed environment has so far been mostly neglected by the research community. Current discussion centres mostly around Cloud Security and Privacy/Data Protection. The impact of forensic investigations on Cloud environments was little noticed.

In 2009, scholars argued that "[...] to their, no research has been published on how cloud computing environments affect digital artifacts, and on acquisition logistics and legal issues related to cloud computing environments." They further debated on, the evolution of technology is some mixed bag economies, but massive investments are being made in Cloud technology.

In the bid to moderate Information Technology exploited by people, which reveals private and professional life, law enforcement officers more and more exploit it for evidence from Cloud environments which is highly significant for litigation or criminal proceedings.

The globalization era provides a new paradigm for criminals and states (state espionage), with security breaches, attacks or policy violations occur, which appeals for necessary digital forensic investigation. However, existing digital forensic principles, frameworks, practices and tools are largely intended for off-line investigation.

It is usually assumed that the storage media under investigation is completely within the control of the investigator. Despite the proliferation of tools, conducting investigations in a cloud computing environment presents new challenges since the evidence is likely to be ephemeral and stored on media beyond the immediate control of an investigator.

B. Challenges Relating to the Operation of Business.

These are key concepts on which the regulation of the business of financial service provision is founded. They include the changing basis of the operation of the economy and new business models.

In the last 30 years, there has been a paradigm shift in the way the economy has been operating, much of it spurred by the internet. The internet was created to reach out to unserved markets, with the message or product largely unchanged. The service or pattern took a different shift from message to mobile phones, combining computer, GPS, research assistant, music player, newspaper, translator and TV'. Millions of smart phone applications are listed in online stores like 'google app'.

As more products become connected to the internet through the Internet of Things (IoT), physical products are set to incorporate more such pervasive add-ons. For example; Cameroonians use their mobile phone to service customers either to transfer data or place calls and mobile money services, enabling the phone subscriber to reach out to a different customer community through banking services under certain conditions (Cheka, 2018).

Conventionally, money and its management has been the business of banks because as credit institutions, banks traditional pattern of storing money in registered cards and servers have adopted a different strategy by cooperating with Mobile Telephone Operators (MTOs) not only to facilitate the communication of data (and semantically speaking, money is data), but by integrating Mobile Financial Services (MFS) into their service platforms.

MTOs are increasingly invading the banking sector through mergers and acquisitions (M&A), buying into the shareholding of banks and entrenchment into digital banking by the reinforcement of their human resource bases through an increasing recruitment of new staff from the traditional banking sector and dark world (some organize hacking and programming competition which recruit young persons in these companies).

The connected digital economy is changing this. Beginning with the computer and moving quickly into smartphones, devices and other objects, the way value is created by the mobile phone customer within their use contexts is changing the mobile phone operator's relationship with the customer into one that is longer, more enduring and intricately linked to other firms.

The use of money stored in the phone as 'data', the customer can make better use of time without leaving their seat and yet inter alia pay bills with utility companies, provide pocket money (mobile money services) to relatives in distant lands, and as well locate eating places.

Most service provider's licence issued by the regulator are on the base on the provision of mobile phone services for making calls and the transfer of 'data' (oblivious of the fact that money too is now stored in the phone as 'data' and eventually used as money). In other words, the dynamism in new business models today constitutes a challenge which the regulator in the licensing of financial service provision must grapple with.

In Cameroon, this challenge is evident in the current multiplicity of money transfer business and tax is creating disputes pitching microfinance institutions such as Express Union and Express Exchange, against Orange and Mobile Telephone Network (MTN) over jurisdiction relating to electronic money transfer activities[8]. Mobile phone operators (MTOs) were initially not involved in money transfer or the mobile money business and microfinance institutions relied on the bandwidth of MTOs to carry out this activity. The recent entry into the electronic money transfer business and tax without much ado on multinational (MTOs) (Orange, Nextel and MTN) is an economic menace to local community.

C. Challenges that Touch on the Ascription of Legal Responsibility.

The digital age has altered aspects of human existence through a subtle revisiting the concepts of time, space and being; all of which, it is submitted, are philosophical notions that lie at the heart of rules relating to fixing of legal responsibility in the provision of financial services (for example the new tax law of mobile transfer). Time, space and being present important similarities, differences and features on questions of the regulation of the quality of evidence like identification and proofs of the violation of rules by operators.

1. Time

Humans in the digital age are in need of time and information as never before. Conventionally, time (Markosian 2003) is a part of the measuring system used to sequence events, to compare the duration of events and the intervals between

8 Ibid

them, and to quantify rates of change such as the motions of objects. The temporal position of events with respect to the transitory present is continually changing; future events become present, then pass further and further into the past. Time is also an expression of the changing state of matter.

Two contrasting viewpoints on time divide many prominent philosophers. One view is that time is part of the fundamental structure of the universe, a dimension in which events occur in sequence. Sir Isaac Newton subscribed to this realist view, and hence this position is often referred to as Newtonian time.

On the contrary, time does not refer to any kind of 'container' that events and objects 'move through', nor to any entity that 'flows', but that it is instead part of a fundamental intellectual structure (together with space and number) within which humans sequence and compare events. This second view holds that time is neither an event nor a thing, and thus is not itself measurable nor can it be travelled.

The foregoing philosophical divide does not, however deter a submission to the effect that, in the digital age, Newtonian time is of the essence in the regulation of provision of financial services. Services in the era of the internet of things are struck by Newtonian time; enabling a buyer, for example, to identify an article displayed on their mobile phone, select, pay for it and direct delivery to their address in real-time by using the same phone through a simple click; all of this without going to the bank (for money with which to pay), the shop (to collect the goods) and even having to meet the courier (to arrange for delivery to their address). This is a contributing factor to social development, as it limits unnecessary occupation of geographical space (high street shopping space), as the seller may only have displayed the article on a URL.

2. Cyber space

The concept of 'space' in the digital age constitutes the law-maker's nightmare. Conventionally, law is passed and enforced within the framework of a fixed and identifiable geographical area primarily on a being who may be a physical or moral person. 'Space' does not however seem so straightforward in the digital age because cyberspace is borderless and regulating it is a quandary.

Notions of national identity grounded in geography is problematized, in relation to the internet (Tofts 2004: 149). The concept of 'space' is scuttled and blunted or obfuscated in the digital age by the apparently elastic and fictional concept of 'virtual space'.

'Virtual space' is a digital or nonphysical environment. It is a phrase that refers to computer-simulated environments that can mimic physical presence in places in the real as well as in imaginary worlds. This simulation is today stretched even further by the creation of a 'being' devoid of the body as well as the acceptance and current use of virtual money such as Bitcoin albeit in the real world.

The Difficulty of Regulating 'Space'

Based on the foregoing, the borderlessness of space creates a lawless cyber space that may be harmful to life in the real world. However, most regional and international organizations have adopted legal regulations and even creating organizations to investigate and prosecute criminals related to any activities as per these laws.

The internet permits the creation of a bodiless 'being', an identity that is used by scammers to exploit the naivety of others. This is in spite of the fact Tofts (2014) claims that 'the duality of actual self and digital representation, or avatar (be it text, graphic or image) is the anchor that smoothes out and reconciles the ambiguous split that seems to occur between the worlds of the body and virtuality when we communicate across a network'. It is, however, submitted that the validity of the claim by Tofts here assumes the creation of innocent and traceable innocuous beings in the cyber world.

Drawing from the case in Cameroon, where national security law is unenforceable on diaspora-based drivers of the on-going conflict in Cameroon's Anglophone regions, because they are bodiless and virtually untraceable, Toft's assertion regarding the duality of actual self is untenable. But the rule of the 'game' has changed, with the arrest of some persons alleged promoters of the Conflict in Nigeria and the issuing of international order against others in Europe.

Today, it is possible to hide the 'body' by using cryptographic dissimulation or veil all traces by using multiple chains, avatars or multiple platforms in the transmission of messages. Evans (2001) discusses this duality in relation to virtual reality.

In Sum Res Cogitans (I am a Thinking Being) Descartes claims that 'I am a being whose whole essence or nature is to think, and whose whole being requires no place and depends on no material living'. This reflects the duality of mind and body which is interesting to consider in relation to virtual reality which is a place for the disembodied mind (Evans 2001:199).

There has always been a connection between the state, politics, trade, security and money; which does not ease the task of its regulation. Based on the 2011-2016 report of the Central Bank of Central African States (BEAC) of which Cameroon is part, mobile money is at the centre of which Cameroon is involved in trade. On the strength of this report, 95 per cent of electronic money transfers were effected through mobile money.

In addition, BEAC has recognized that mobile money is a tool for financial inclusion, which is still clogged by some regulatory setbacks. This, to quote the Governor of BEAC, is, however, because, 'innovations always precede legal framework'.

As of March 21, 2018, BEAC was in the process of fine-tuning the legal framework on new rules governing mobile money transactions 'which will include the fight against money laundering' This is especially because trade and globalization, that are otherwise legitimate, provide a conduit for money laundering and the financing of terrorism. The regulation of financial service provision must strike a balance that facilitates globalized trade without jeopardizing the security of the state or trade-based money laundering (TBML).

With the improvement in the technology of data collection, serious concerns emerge about their potential misuse such as the invasion of the user's privacy by hackers. This is because the internet functions by sending data from computer to computer in bundles or packets until the data reaches its destination. Anything could happen to this bundle in the process as the Snowden disclosures or the Cambridge Analytica data harvesting scandal have shown. In this way, almost all personal information is available online and can be used and abused without difficulty by the tech-savvy.

CHAPTER TWO

TECHNOLOGY INNOVATION AND FORENSICS

The 9/11 events like no other in the world, re-oriented security strategy around the globe, pulling in new fields like criminal profiling, forensic investigation and counter-terrorism machinery; like drones. The prime focus of this chapter is to examine a number of security technologies that may threaten an "evidence blackout" and consequences. The technologies which are to be analyzed are: full disk encryption, secure network communication, secure processors, homomorphic encryption and anonymous routing.

Encryption

Encryption is a word which is common to hackers, programmers and cyber security analyst. Encryption technologies are typically based on the idea of computational security, cryptanalysis which requires infeasible amounts of computing expertise or lengths of time. The existence of computing expertise able to tackle current cyphers in a meaningful time-scale is not acknowledged by those likely to possess them. Encryption has thus reached the point of being "practically unbreakable".

Full Disk Encryption (FDE)

Current digital forensic techniques depend largely on artefacts left behind on disk, both explicitly, and as a by-product by the operating system. The first "dark cloud" on the horizon is that, these techniques do not perform well when faced with serious attempts at concealment by encrypting full disks.

Full disk encryption allows the entire contents of a disk to be protected by a password/key scheme, which necessitates the forensic investigator to either have the key or have hacking skills to access the contents of the disk. To achieve this, a layer is introduced into the Operating System between the file system and storage media device driver. Any data being written to the disk is encrypted on-the-fly as it passes through this layer. Conversely, any data being read is decrypted, provided that the correct decryption key has been provided at the beginning of a session.

The advantage of such a scheme is that it is largely transparent to the user — no special actions are required to conceal particular items of data as everything is automatically encrypted/decrypted. Popular implementations of this technology include VeraCrypt and Bitlocker.

Technical Issues related to digital forensics

One of the major framing of digital investigations are control of forensic evidence data. From the technical point of view, this evidence data can be available in three different states: at rest, in motion or in execution.

Data at rest is represented by allocated disk space (Birk, 2011). Whether the data is stored in a database or in a specific file format, it allocates disk space (with computer persons usually refer to as partition of the computer space).

Furthermore, if a file is deleted, the disk space is de-allocated for the operating system but the data is still accessible since the disk space has not been re-allocated and overwritten[9]. This fact is often exploited by investigators which explore these de-allocated disk space on hard-disks. There exists several software which investigators, forensic investigators exploit to recover deleted files.

In case the data is in motion, data is transferred from one entity to another, for example; a typical file transfer over a network can be seen as a data in motion scenario. Several encapsulated protocols contain the data each leaving specific traces on systems and network devices which can in return be used by investigators.

Data can be loaded into memory and executed as a process. In this case, the data is neither at rest or in motion but in execution. On the executing system, process information, machine instruction and allocated/de-allocated data can be analyzed by creating a snapshot of the current system state.

Sources and Nature of Evidence

Concerning the technical aspects of forensic investigations, the amount of potential evidence available to the investigator strongly diverges between the different Cloud service and deployment models. Independently from the used model, the following three components could act as sources for potential evidential data.

Virtual Cloud Instance

The virtual instance within the cloud, where i.e. data is stored or processes are handled, provides potential evidence. In most of the cases, it is the place where an incident happened

9 http://www.sodocs.net/doc/44119f5da9956bec0975f46527d3240c8547a159.html

and hence provides a potential starting point for a forensic investigation. The instance can be accessed by both, the CSP and the customer who is running the instance.

Snapshots provide a powerful technique for the customer to freeze specific states of the virtual machine. Therefore, virtual instances can be still running which leads to the case of live investigations or can be turned off leading to static image analysis. In SaaS and PaaS scenarios, the ability to access the virtual instance for gathering evidential information is highly limited or simply not possible.

Network Layer

The different ISO/OSI network layers provide several information on protocols and communication between instances within the cloud as well as with instances outside the cloud. Unfortunately, ordinary CSP currently do not provide any log data from the network components. This means, that in case of malware infection of an IaaS VM, it will be difficult to get any form of routing information. This situation gets even more complicated in case of PaaS or SaaS. Hence, the situation of forensic evidence is again strongly affected by the support the investigator receives from the customer and the CSP.

Client System

On the system layer of the client, it completely depends on the used model (IaaS, PaaS, SaaS) if and where potential evidence could be extracted. In most of the Cloud scenarios, the browser on the client system is the only application that communicates with the service in the cloud. This especially holds for SaaS applications which are used and controlled by the web browser. Hence, in an exhaustive forensic investigation, the evidence data gathered from the browser environment should not be omitted.

Despite this technological revolution, states, private and international organizations continue to develop new strategies to combat emerging menace on cloud services. From partnership to sharing of intelligence, to conferences, criminals are increasingly apprehended.

Chapter Three

Simulating And Investigating Criminal Activities Using Cloud

The world is a global village, each point connected to one another, just with a click one can access information about an individual or state. There has been a paradigm shift from analog to digital has not only boosted the economy of states and cooperate organization, but that of individuals. Who say innovation, equally talks of challenges, these boost has also paved the way for criminals, who exploit such services to swindle funds from individuals, states, and organizations, some states equally exploit these technologies against other states, information is being weaponized.

In this chapter, will not only be focus on the simulation of criminal case on the cloud, but how to investigate such case and how some criminals operate before and after exploiting a device.

Examining Case 009

One of the first activity to do when on a criminal scene is to document the pattern or collect critical analysis on ground intelligence. Each country has a department in the police, which exploit crime scene, as well as a forensic department, as such they usually collect and gather the evidence, document it according to applicable procedural and legal requirements.

Using case 009 as an example, to provide the necessary steps to be taken when investigating a criminal act, is provided below. For proper criminal investigation, the law enforcement officer must exploit record of the location and original condition of the devices of assume suspect (case 009). The following are examples for proper documentation of the scene:

- Laptop computer: evidence number EVI001
- Tablette: evidence number EVI001A
- Internet Modem: EVI001B
- Internal hard drive: evidence number EVI001C
- USB Thumb drive: evidence number EVI001D
- DVD: evidence number EVI001E

Its usually challenging for law enforcement officers to locate, apprehend and exploit materials or tools of criminals. As most of them after using these tools, sometimes sell to the dark market and purchase new devices or tools. This is essential fact for investigators, because the possibility of seizing only devices that contain information to be assessed, documenting the effects that have been reviewed might re-orient the case. Devices that contain data to be analyzed like internal hard disks, thumb drives and DVDs, can be compromised, laptop and internet modem without the above elements lacks useful information, upon reflection of suspect 009 case (after perpetrating a crime, devices or tools are sold to the dark market).

Critically, internet modems are more and more exploited by criminals, suspect 009 might be using a crack modem (which takes any SIM card), which is identified with someone else's name (exploit service providers of mobile service operators. By telling the agent, his identity card is missing or pay high for the Sim card to be registered with the agent's name), and the modem usually has an input memory, which some insert a memory card and access critical information about their deals. Scholars argue that, with the development of new techniques, with an IMEI, of any device, a criminal can be trace, but there exist methods of changing these numbers.

However, some devices can be avoided to be transported and stored, because of inadequate data. But is needs to be assessed by a specialist since the intervened effects may have some kind of technical relationship with the device exploited and without which it would not be possible to analyze properly. For each device, the following data must be documented:

- Type: Computer, hard drive, flash drive, DVD.
- Brand and model.
- Storage capacity, indicating if it is MB, GB or TB.
- Serial number.
- State: Damaged, on, off, etc.
- Location: Stay and specific place.
- Security: Access password, PIN.
- Comments: Used only by children, not connected to the internet.

Moreover, any annotation related to the use of passwords, settings, email accounts, as well as the SIM cardholders with their ICCID, original PIN and PUK number and any other relevant information that may be searched will be searched and documented. They will be used in the subsequent analysis of the devices.

Investigations in XaaS Environments

With continuous synergy and sharing of information and trainings by international criminal police (Interpol) in Europe, the West and Africa, new techniques of investigations have been developed in relation to SaaS, PaaS and IaaS environments.

1. SaaS Environments

The SaaS model, limits discretion of the customer, as the latter cannot access or control operating infrastructure such as network, servers, operating systems and application that is been exploited. This simply means customer has no insight of the system and service it provides. Only limited user-specific application configuration settings can be controlled. Its sometime challenging as the investigator has to rely on high-level logs which are eventually provided by the CSP. The CSP does not run any logging application, the customer has no opportunity to create any useful evidence by himself. The installation or configuration of any toolkit or logging tool is impossible.

Despite the above control of the model, even a forensic investigation has limited techniques to recover after strict scan of tools, and which only leads to the assumption that customers of SaaS models do not have any chance to analyze potential incidences.

Moreover, evidence data which need to be interpreted by an investigator, will be challenging due to lack of circumstantial information. For auditors, this situation does not change, as questions on who accessed specific data and information cannot be answered by the customers, if no corresponding logs are available.

Moreover, a lot of SaaS CSP like Google offer Single sign-on (SSO) access control to the complete set of their services. Unfortunately, in case of an account breach, most of the CSP do not offer any possibility for the customer to identify which data and information has been accessed by the adversary.

In private SaaS, the scenario is different, for the fact that the customer and the CSP are probably under the same authority. The logging mechanisms could be implemented which contribute to potential investigations. Thereby providing the exact location of the servers and the data is known at any time.

The limited ability of receiving forensic information from the server in SaaS scenarios, appeals on the support of the client in the process. This can be achieved by implementing Proofs of Retrievability (POR) in which a verifier (client) is enabled to determine that a prover (server) possesses a file or data object without actually downloading it.

2. PaaS Environments

The Paas has a core advantage to the customer, as the application is under his or her control. Given these circumstances, the customer obtains theoretically the power to dictate how the application interacts with other dependencies (databases, storage entities). Moreover, depending on the runtime environment, logging mechanisms can be implemented which automatically sign the information and transfer it to a third party storage.

The major technique to isolate criminal patterns is encryption, as it helps prevent potential interception or hackers to easily access log data information on the way to storage server. CSP usually claim that, data transfer is encrypted, is yet to be verified, as most customers interact with the platform over a prepared API, system states and specific application logs can be extracted. However potential adversaries, which can lead to system or application breach, should not be able to alter these log files afterwards which could be realized by push-only mechanisms.

Unfortunately, the customer has no direct control of the underlying runtime environment. As in the SaaS scenario, this strongly depends on the configuration done by the CSP. Concerning the Microsoft Azure platform, the environment is made of a virtualized OS (Microsoft Windows), a webserver (Internet Information Server) and the runtime environment (.NET). Windows Azure Diagnostics, a new feature released in November 2009, gives developers the ability to collect and store a variety of diagnostics data in a highly configurable way.

3. IaaS Environments

Forensic investigation and cloud computing are strategic issues which continue to be table during international, regional and national security conferences on cyber security and counter terrorism. Drawing from a forensic point of view, IaaS instances provide much more information that could exploited as forensic evidence in case of an incident than the PaaS and SaaS models do (ENISA, 2016)[10]. Simply because there that ability of the customer to install and set up the image for forensic purposes. Hence, log data and other evidence information could be transferred to other hosts in a frequent manner for providing the ability to perform an investigation whenever needed.

Snapshots

Traditional forensics expect target machines to be powered down to collect an image. This situation completely changed with the advent of the snapshot method which is supported by all popular hypervisors such as Xen, VMware ESX and

10 ENISA, ,2016. Exploring Cloud Incidents, TLP GREEN | JUNE 2016

Hyper-V1. Snapshots, also referred to as forensic image, of virtual machines provide a powerful tool with which a virtual machine can be cloned by one click including also the running system's memory. This leads to the main benefit that systems hosting crucial business processes do not have to be shut down for performing a forensic analysis. This could also affect scenarios in which a downtime of a system is not feasible or practical due to existing SLAs.

Due to the fact that the customer is responsible for the security of the virtual instance, the system itself can be prepared for forensic investigation purposes. RFC 3227 contains several best practices for responding to a security incident especially in the case of live investigating systems.

According to, log data information concerning currently logged users, open ports, running processes, system and registry information etc. should be gathered. These log data should be transferred to an external system mitigating the chance that a maliciously motivated shutdown process destroys the data. Encrypting and signing these log files can be helpful for providing security and integrity of the created log files.

Unfortunately, it has to be emphasized that each process such as an encryption process run on the virtual instance, can be controlled by the hypervisor or the CSP respectively. Although this risk can be disregarded in most of the cases, the impact on the security of high security environments is tremendous.

Generally, for an investigator it is important to know if the virtual machine was properly shutdown or is still running. Hence, virtual instances have to be divided into two different categories concerning the forensic analysis of the system: shutdown (dead) and running (live) virtual systems. In general, live investigations on running virtual machines become more common providing evidence data that is not available on shutdown systems.

The technique of live investigation is mostly influenced by the huge amount of evidence data that has to be stored and processed in case of shutdown instances. Nevertheless, it cannot be denied that live investigations change the state of the investigated system and the results of the investigation may not be repeatable. However, this does not prevent a lot of SMCs from mostly performing live investigations due to the bond of legislation and government-contracting agreements.

Volatile Data

There is no doubt that forensic investigation is necessary when cloud computing service has been compromised. From the analysis above there is equally no debate that virtual IaaS instances do not have any persistent storage. With an AWS. EC2 cloud instance, all volatile data is lost if the instance is rebooted or shutdown. Data need to be stored or preserved in long time storage environments like Amazon Simple Storage Service (S3) or Amazon Elastic Block Store (EBS).

This scenario is crucial, in case an adversary compromises a virtual IaaS instance with no persistent storage synchronization, the adversary could shutdown the system leading to a complete loss of volatile data. More so, the instance could be exploited to send spam, attack further external and internal targets, join botnets and steal volatile data of the running system. After the attack, the attacker can cancel the contract with the corresponding CSP forcing the virtual machine to shutdown and destroy most of the evidence data which is inevitable for further forensic investigations. This problem mainly results from the unclear situation how CSP handle the termination of customer contracts.

In recent times, this process is not transparent for the customer bringing up further questions, as data on virtual systems in the cloud get exhaustively deleted and how it's done? File deletion is all about control and this used to not be an issue till the advent of Cloud Computing.

In current Cloud environments CSP do not offer any verification process providing the ability for the customer to verify that the sensitive data stored on a virtual machine has been deleted exhaustively.

Moreover, an interesting perspective is the case in which the real owner of the image decides to engage in malicious activities through his EC2 machine from a veiled IP address and afterwards claims, someone compromised the password or key pair to his EC2 machine. In a subsequent forensic investigation, it will be difficult to prove the opposite due to the lack of evidences.

Virtual Introspection

Everything connected to the internet can be hacked or have been hacked or even compromised, the Amazon EC2 instances in the end of 2009, is a perfect example. However, this has led to development of new security domains, like forensic investigation and the reconceptualization of the notion of hacking, and other IT related fields, to help determine how defend virtual environment menace and to exploit how systems have been compromised and recovering process can be effectuated.

Virtual Introspection (VI) is the process by which the state of a virtual machine is observed from either the VMM or from some virtual machines other than the one being examined. However, the fact that the VMM has full access to the resources of all VMs represents a significant risk to customers' data. The issue whether VMs can ever be managed by a VMM, while simultaneously being protected from a compromised VMM remains an open research problem.

Securing network communication

The 21st century is that of cyber war, where each country needs to secure its network communication and transfer of strategic data related to national security. Transnational actors like other petit hackers continue to aspire to compromised pertinent communication transmissions, even organizations hire hackers for industrial espionage. The transmission of strongly encrypted messages, by states, military and intelligence services is within the grasp of both the ordinary citizen, and the criminal. HTTP Secure (HTTPS), Virtual Private Network (VPN), Internet Protocol Security (IPSec) and all have achieved widespread adoption.

1. **Secure Processors**

Secure processor technology promises to do for memory image forensics what full disk encryption did for disk examination, render it impossible. In a system with a secure processor, all data outside the boundary of the processor itself, this means everything in random access memory (RAM), is encrypted. Both program instructions and data are decrypted on-the-fly with block ciphers as data is shifted to and from the various system buses.

Systems such as Aegis and Bastion, use to secure processors were originally intended to provide a secure environment for embedded control systems but continue to develop towards high-end systems. Most Sub Saharan African countries have adopted it for desktop level systems.

2. **Anonymous Routing**

Following the nature of the protocols underlying the operation of the internet, it is possible to identify the source and destination of network traffic. Even if encryption is in place, it is thus possible to establish that two parties are in communication.

The advent of anonymous routing (onion routing as embodied in the Onion Router (TOR protocol) removes this source of evidence. The TOR works by separating the concerns of identity and routing. It forwards messages randomly though a network of TOR servers (nodes), with each one applying a layer of encryption (hence the onion metaphor) before forwarding the packet to the next node or ultimately its intended destination. This prevents both the source and destination of the message from being known by every node and prevents traffic analysis.

Whilst current onion routing implementations have their weaknesses (various attacks against the anonymity have been demonstrated), systems such as the TOR network have demonstrated their viability. Such techniques are available to those with sufficient knowledge and reason to hide the origin and destination of their incoming and outgoing data.

Chapter Four

Collection And Handling Of Digital Evidence

There is no doubt that security is a process, from criminal profiling, investigating the suspect, apprehending and handling a crime scene or forensic evidence material to be exploited. The collection and handling of digital evidence, require strategic principles, here are some of the rule used for specific devices.

Collecting and handling digital evidence when a device is on

a) When the device or equipment is on, do not turn it off.

Verify installation of anti-forensic systems: identify remote programs, like logic bomb, and external access.

In case with laptop machine abort processes by pulling the power cable or removing the battery if necessary.

Isolate the device from the networks to which it is connected unless you are authorized to access cloud services[11].

11 Read, Interpol's; GUIDELINES FOR DIGITAL FORENSICS FIRST RESPONDERS Best practices for search and seizure of electronic and digital evidence March 2021

Disable screensavers and screen locking in order to prevent the equipment from being hibernated or suspended.

Verify if the device has any kind of encryption system running (Bitlocker, FileVault, VeraCrypt, PGP Disk, etc.).

Collecting and handling digital evidence when a device is power off

b) When the equipment is turned off, do not turn it on until it is processed with guarantees, as further explained later.

Most countries the legislator did not provide any principle should in case where a device is requisition and whether the suspect's password/pin must be requested verified or make use of hacker to access the device. An example is the request of the Federal Bureau of Investigation (FBI) for a hacker to unlock a phone of a criminal (the San Bernardino Case).

Procedure for handling digital evidence of a criminal act

Drawing from the narrative of international criminal police and other regional and national organizations, several actions have been adopted, which are but not limited to:

1. **Seizure**

One of the first move of law enforcement officers when investigating and after apprehending a suspect, is to seize any device in his or her possession, document, described and sealed, while leaving the decision for further analysis to the criminal justice system or judiciary. The seize device can only be exploited after being unsealed by competent authority.

2. Generate a forensic copy

More and more with technological evolution, most police stations have forensic investigators, as such, to generate forensic evidence on a scene, the investigator will simply describe specific procedures by documentation. Some of the procedure used are, but not limited to; cloned, image or any other system used.

3. Tools

Tools here simply refer to hardware duplicator, write blocker, software, but is appropriate to equally mention that it can be channeled to different location with the use of disk, file with data obtained from a telephone.

4. HASH and Observations

Most devices have an Algorithm used and the signature which can be obtained. Observation simply focus on any incident which may arise during the copy process.

Conclusion

With the emergence of new technologies and services, such as Cloud Computing, several companies benefit from its security and help minimize budgets for security resources. However, regarding digital forensics, the loss of control caused by Cloud environments and vendors presents a huge challenge for investigators. There is need to rethink the procedure and exploitation method of digital forensics. Investigators need to be enforce through capacity building programs in order to incorporate the fast fluctuating world of Cloud Computing.

Scholars and experts in the field of security studies have posed several questions in order to understand, what collateral data the investigator can identify and collect to help him prove or disprove the hypothesis. Is there any knowledge about what the CSP logs and how long he keeps this information? Does the CSP vouch for the integrity of the evidential data? Currently, customers have to accept that evidential artifacts of digital investigations in Cloud environments will be unreliable and incomplete.

Considering the concessions made by the CSP through SLAs or other forms of contracts, it is almost impossible for the customer to verify this. Suppose that a customer made a contract with a CSP which guarantees data redundancy for the customer data. How can the customer prove that this agreement is fulfilled? However, these reasons are not the only ones making Cloud Computing a complex issue for digital investigations.

The absence of a standard for processes within the Cloud and the Cloud in general causes a lot of problems ranging from security, compliance and proper deployment to the question of how an investigation within such an environment shall be processed. When new standards or adjustments to existing standards are needed, as it is the case with Cloud Computing, creating too many standards should be avoided. Standards have to promote innovation and do not inhibit it.

Finally, there is also the need for the digital forensics community to establish standard empirical mechanisms to evaluate frameworks, procedures and software tools for use in a cloud environment. Only when research has been conducted to show the true impact of the cloud on digital forensics, can we be sure how to alter and develop alternative frameworks and guidelines as well as tools to combat crimes in the cloud[12].

12 Read George Grispos's, Calm Before the Storm: The Challenges of Cloud Computing in Digital Forensics.

Reference

Cheka, C. (2018) Challenges of Regulating Financial Service Provision in Cameroon in the Digital Age and a Globalized World. Africa Development, Volume XLIII, No. 2, 2018, pp. 85-106. Council for the Development of Social Science Research in Africa, 2019 (ISSN: 0850 3907)

National Research Council, Strengthening Forensic Science in the United States: A Path Forward. Washington, DC: National Academies Press, 2009.

President's Council of Advisors on Science and Technology, Report to the President Forensic Science in Criminal Courts: Ensuring Scientific Validity of Feature-Comparison Methods. Washington, DC: Executive Office of the President, 2016.

D. M. Risinger, M. J. Saks, W. C. Thompson, and R. Rosenthal, "The Daubert/Kumho implications of observer effects in forensic science: hidden problems of expectation and suggestion," California Law Review, vol. 90, no. 1, 2002.

P. Roberts, "Paradigms of forensic science and legal process: a critical diagnosis," Philosophical Transactions of the Royal Society B, vol. 370, no. 1674, article no. 20140256, 2015.

M. Meyers and M. Rogers, "Digital forensics: meeting the challenges of scientific evidence," in IFIP International

Conference on Digital Forensics. Boston, MA: Springer, 2005, pp. 43-50.

E. Van Buskirk and V. T. Liu, "Digital evidence: challenging the presumption of reliability," Journal of Digital Forensic Practice, vol. 1, no. 1, pp. 19-26, 2006.

G. Edmond and D. Mercer, "Trashing junk science," Stanford Technology Law Review, no. 3, 1998.

R. G. Behrents, "Lucy fell from a tree and plunged 40 feet to her death," American Journal of Orthodontics and Dentofacial Orthopedics, vol. 150, no. 5, pp. 719-722, 2016.

H. F. Fradella, A. Fogarty, and L. O'Neill, "The impact of Daubert on the admissibility of behavioral sciencetestimony," Pepperdine Law Review, vol. 30, no. 3, pp. 403-444, 2002.

D. J. Ryan and G. Shpantzer, "Legal aspects of digital forensics," 2002 [Online]. Available:http://euro.ecom.cmu.edu/program/law/08-732/Evidence/RyanShpantzer.pdf.

D. B. Garrie, "Digital forensic evidence in the courtroom: understandingcontentandquality," NorthwesternJournal of Technology and Intellectual Property, vil. 12, no. 2, article no. 5, 2014.

S. Mahle, "An introduction to Daubert v. Merrell Dow," 2008 [Online]. Available: http://www.daubertexpert.com/basics_daubert-v-merrell-dow.html.

European Network of Forensic Science Institutes, "Best Practice Manual for the forensic examination of handwriting," Report No. ENFSI-BPM-FHX-01, 2015.

S. Garfinkel, P. Farrell, V. Roussev, and G. Dinolt, "Bringing science to digital forensics with standardized forensic corpora," Digital Investigation, vol. 6, pp. S2-S11, 2009.

I. Baggili and F. Breitinger, "Data sources for advancing cyber forensics: what the social world has to offer,"in Proceedings of the 2015 AAAI Spring Symposium Series, Palo Alto, CA, 2015.

R. Bekkerman, "Automatic categorization of email into folders: benchmark experiments on Enron and SRIcorpora," University of Massachusetts Amherst, MA, 2004.

MAWI Working Group Traffic Archive [Online]. Available: http://mawi.wide.ad.jp/mawi/.

H. Visti, "ForGe: computer forensic test image generator," 2013 [Online]. Available: https://articles.forensicfocus.com/2013/10/18/forge-computer-forensic-test-image-generator/

M. Powell, "The canterbury corpus," 2001 [Online]. Available: http://corpus.canterbury.ac.nz/.

Alexandru Iacob, Lucian Itu, Lucian Sasu, Florin Moldoveanu, and Constantin Suciu. Gpu accelerated information retrieval using bloom filters. In System Theory, Control and Computing (ICSTCC), 2015 19th International Conference on, pages 872–876. IEEE, 2015.

Arijit Ukil, Jaydip Sen, and Sripad Koilakonda.

Ben Hitchcock, Nhien-An Le-Khac, and Mark Scanlon. Tiered forensic methodology model for digital field triage by non-digital evidence specialists. Digital Investigation, 13(S1), 03 2016. Proceedings of the Third Annual DFRWS Europe.

Darren Quick and Kim-Kwang Raymond Choo. Impacts of increasing volume of digital forensic data: A survey and future research challenges. Digital Investigation, 11(4): 273–294, 2014.

E. Morioka and M.S. Sharbaf. Cloud computing: Digital forensic solutions. In Information Technology - New Generations (ITNG), 2015 12th International Conference on, pages 589–594, April 2015.

Embedded security for Internet of Things. In 2011 2nd National Conference on Emerging Trends and Applications in Computer Science, pages 1–6. IEEE, mar 2011. ISBN 978-1-4244-9578-8.

Frank Breitinger and Vassil Roussev. Automated evaluation of approximate matching algorithms on real data. Digital Investigation, 11:S10–S17, 2014.

Garda Síochána Inspectorate. Changing Policing in Ireland, November 2015.

George W. Furnas, Thomas K. Landauer, Louis M. Gomez, and Susan T. Dumais. The vocabulary problem in human-system communication. Communications of the ACM, 30(11):964–971, 1987.

Guangxuan Chen, Yanhui Du, Panke Qin, and Jin Du. Suggestions to digital forensics in cloud computing era. In Network Infrastructure and Digital Content (ICNIDC), 2012 3rd IEEE International Conference on, pages 540–544, Sept 2012.

Iain Sutherland, Huw Read, and Konstantinos Xynos. Forensic analysis of smart TV: A current issue and call to arms. Digital Investigation, 11(3):175–178, sep 2014.

Ibrahim Baggili, Jeff Oduro, Kyle Anthony, Frank Breitinger, and Glenn McGee. Watch What You Wear: Preliminary

Forensic Analysis of Smart Watches. In 2015 10th International Conference on Availability, Reliability and Security, pages 303–311. IEEE, aug 2015. ISBN 978-1-4673-6590-1.

Jason Power, Yinan Li, Mark D Hill, Jignesh M Patel, and David A Wood. Toward gpus being mainstream in analytic processing. 2015.

Joshua I James and Yunsik Jake Jang. Measuring digital crime investigation capacity to guide international crime prevention strategies. In Future Information Technology, pages 361–366. Springer, 2014.

Juniper Research. The Internet of Things: Consumer, Industrial & Public Services 2015-2020, July 2015.

Kathryn Watkins, Mike McWhorte, Jeff Long, and Bill Hill. Teleporter: An analytically and forensically sound duplicate transfer system. Digital investigation, 6:S43–S47, 2009.

Keyun Ruan, Joe Carthy, Tahar Kechadi, and Ibrahim Baggili. Cloud forensics definitions and critical criteria for cloud forensic capability: An overview of survey results. Digital Investigation, 10(1):34 – 43, 2013.

Kulesh Shanmugasundaram, Nasir Memon, Anubhav Savant, and Herve Bronnimann. Fornet: A distributed forensics network. In Computer Network Security, pages 1–16. Springer, 2003.

Lei Chen, Lanchuan Xu, Xiaohui Yuan, and N. Shashidhar. Digital forensics in social networks and the cloud: Process, approaches, methods, tools, and challenges. In Computing, Networking and Communications (ICNC), 2015 International Conference on, pages 1132– 1136, Feb 2015.

Lodovico Marziale, Golden G Richard, and Vassil Roussev. Massive threading: Using gpus to increase the performance of digital forensics tools. digital investigation, 4:73–81, 2007.

Mark Scanlon and M-Tahar Kechadi. Digital evidence bag selection for p2p network investigation. In Proceedings of the 7th International Symposium on Digital Forensics and Information Security (DFIS- 2013), pages 307–314. Springer, Gwangju, South Korea, 2014.

Mohammad Wazid, Avita Katal, RH Goudar, and Smitha Rao. Hacktivism trends, digital forensic tools and challenges: A survey. In Information & Communication Technologies (ICT), 2013 IEEE Conference on, pages 138–144. IEEE, 2013.

Neha Thethi and Anthony Keane. Digital forensics investigations in the cloud. In IEEE International Advance Computing Conference (IACC), Sept 2012.

Nickson M Karie and Hein S Venter. Taxonomy of challenges for digital

forensics. Journal of forensic sciences, 60(4):885–893, 2015.

Nicole Beebe and Glenn Dietrich. A new process model for text string searching. In Advances in Digital Forensics III, pages 179–191. Springer, 2007.

Nicole Beebe. Digital forensic research: The good, the bad and the unaddressed. In Advances in digital forensics V, pages 17– 36. Springer, 2009.

Nicole Lang Beebe and Jan Guynes Clark. Digital forensic text string searching:

Improving information retrieval effectiveness by thematically clustering search results. Digital Investigation, 4(SUPPL.):49–54, 2007.

Nicole Lang Beebe and Lishu Liu. Ranking algorithms for digital forensic string search hits. Digital Investigation, 11(SUPPL. 2):314–322, 2014.

Nicole Lang Beebe, Jan Guynes Clark, Glenn B. Dietrich, Myung S. Ko, and Daijin Ko. Post-retrieval search hit clustering to improve information retrieval effectiveness: Two digital forensics case studies. Decision Support Systems, 51(4):732–744, 2011.

NIST. NIST cloud computing forensic science challenges. 2014.

Paul Henry, Jacob Williams, and Benjamin Wright. The sans survey of digital forensics and incident response. In Tech Rep, July 2013.

RB van Baar, HMA van Beek, and EJ van Eijk. Digital forensics as a service: A game changer. Digital Investigation, 11:S54–S62, 2014.

Ricardo Campos, Gaël Dias, Alípio M Jorge, and Adam Jatowt. Survey of temporal information retrieval and related applications. ACM Computing Surveys (CSUR), 47(2):15, 2014.

Robert C. Hegarty, David J. Lamb, and Andrew Attwood. Interoperability Challenges in the Internet of Things. In Paul Dowland, Steven Furnell, and Bogdan Ghita, editors, Proceedings of the Tenth International Network Conference (INC2014), pages 163–172. Plymouth University, 2014.

S. Almulla, Y. Iraqi, and A. Jones. Cloud forensics: A research perspective. In

Innovations in Information Technology (IIT), 2013 9th International Conference on, pages 66–71, March 2013.

Sebastian Breß, Stefan Kiltz, and Martin Schäler. Forensics on gpu coprocessing in databases–research challenges, first experiments, and countermeasures. In BTW Workshops, pages 115–129. Citeseer, 2013.

Simson Garfinkel, Paul Farrell, Vassil Roussev, and George Dinolt. Bringing science to digital forensics with standardized forensic corpora. Digital investigation, 6:S2–S11, 2009.

Simson L Garfinkel. Digital forensics research: The next 10 years. digital investigation, 7: S64–S73, 2010.

Sriram Raghavan. Digital forensic research: current state of the art. CSI Transactions on ICT, 1(1):91–114, 2013.

Stavros Simou, Christos Kalloniatis, Evangelia Kavakli, and Stefanos Gritzalis. Cloud forensics solutions: A review. In Lazaros Iliadis, Michael Papazoglou, and KlausPohl, editors, Advanced Information Systems Engineering Workshops, volume 178 of Lecture Notes in Business Information Processing, pages 299–309. Springer International Publishing, 2014. ISBN 978-3-319-07868-7.

Sylvain Collange, Yoginder S Dandass, Marc Daumas, and David Defour. Using graphics processors for parallelizing hash-based data carving. In System Sciences, 2009. HICSS'09. 42nd Hawaii International Conference on, pages 1–10. IEEE, 2009.

Vassil Roussev and Golden G Richard III. Breaking the performance wall: The case for distributed digital forensics. In Proceedings of the 2004 digital forensics research workshop, volume 94, 2004.

Vassil Roussev, Candice Quates, and Robert Martell. Real-time digital forensics and triage. Digital Investigation, 10(2):158–167, 2013.

Xinyan Zha and Sartaj Sahni. Fast in-place file carving for digital forensics. In Forensics in Telecommunications, Information, and Multimedia, pages 141–158. Springer, 2011.

Yoan Chabot, Aurélie Bertaux, Tahar Kechadi, and Christophe Nicolle. Event reconstruction: A state of the art. Handbook of Research on Digital Crime, Cyberspace Security, and Information Assurance, page 15, 2014.

Ziming Zhong, Vladimir Rychkov, and Alexey Lastovetsky. Data partitioning on heterogeneous multicore and multi-gpu systems using functional performance models of data-parallel applications. In Cluster Computing (CLUSTER), 2012 IEEE International Conference on, pages 191–199. IEEE, 2012.

Arshad, H. et al 2018. Digital Forensics: Review of Issues in Scientific Validation of Digital Evidence. Journal of Information Processing Systems. Volume 14, No 2 (2018), pp. 346 – 376

Paul, A. et al 2012. Cyber Forensics in Cloud Computing. Computer Engineering and Intelligent Systems. Vol 3, No.2, 2012. https://iiste.org/Journals/index.php/CEIS/article/viewFile/982/902/

D. Birk, 2011. echnical Challenges of Forensic Investigations in CloudComputing Environments. https://cachin.com/cc/csc2011/submissions/birk.pdf

A. Wayne, Jansen, NIST, Cloud Hooks: Security and Privacy Issues in Cloud Computing, Proceeding of the 44th

International Conference on System Science, (2011), 1-10. doi:10.1109/HICSS.2011.103

"TOR," Online,https://www.torproject.org/ (downloaded April 2013).

J. J. Roberts, "The FBI Can't Open the Phone of the Texas Church Shooter Devin Kelley, note=http://fortune.com/2017/11/08/ texas-church-shooting-fbi-phone/, accessed november 8 2017,," 2017.

J. Rubin, J. Queally, and P. Dave, "FBI unlocks San Bernardino shooter's iPhone and ends legal battle with Apple, for now," 2016, march 28 http://www.latimes.com/local/lanow/la-me-ln-fbidrops-fight-to-force-apple-to-unlock-san-bernardino-terrorist-iphone-20160328-story.html

Masnick, "Theresa May Tries To Push Forward With Plans To Kill Encryption, While Her Party Plots Via Encrypted WhatsApp," 12 June 2017, https://www.techdirt.com/articles/20170611/11545237565/theresa-may-tries-to-push-forward-with-plans-to-kill-encryptionwhile-her-party-plots-via-encrypted-whatsapp.shtml

"VeraCrypt," https://veracrypt.codeplex.com/

"BitLocker," https://docs.microsoft.com/enus/windows/devicesecurity/bitlocker/bitlocker-overview

R. L. Rivest, L. Adleman, and M. L. Dertouzos, "On data banks and privacy homomorphisms," Foundations of secure computation, vol. 4, no. 11, 1978, pp. 169–180.

S. L. Garfinkel, "Digital forensics research: The next 10 years," Digital Investigation, vol. 7, 2010, pp. S64–S73.

D. Catteddu, "Cloud Computing: benefits, risks and recommendations for information security," in Web application security. Springer, 2010, pp. 17–17.

Index